KRISTA O'REILLY·

About Krista

In the past seven years Krista returned to school, started writing, launched babies into the world as she launched a new business, struggled with fear, anxiety and suicidal thoughts but also learned to ask for help and advocate for her needs.

She walked through surgery, chronic pain, and was diagnosed with an autoimmune disease. She has practiced embracing the truth of what she wants, learned to honor her wiring, and to shore up leaky boundaries. She buried several people she loved, said yes to adventure, worked really hard and gave herself permission to rest. She put down deep, strong roots of self-awareness and self-compassion.

And she picked up joy along the way. Enough to share.

Krista lives in central Alberta, Canada, and works as a writer & Joyful Living Educator. She helps "messy humans" like herself quiet the noise of perfectionism, comparison and fear to show up fully to their imperfect and beautiful lives.

Her message can be summed up in the following simple statements: you're imperfect; life is messy; show up anyway. She'll help you figure out how.

WHY SEASONAL JOURNALING?

It's human to experience ebb and flow in life. We move through seasons of transition and uncertainty; we tilt between self-confidence and self-doubt; we experience shifting levels of energy or productivity and changes in what we need or want.

We witness death and new life.

Life is messy. And beautiful.

Living awake and seasonally allows us to live grateful for the gifts in every season. It means consciously and stubbornly mining for these gifts.

Because there is wisdom knit into the fabric of every season.
Into the light and the dark.

Tuning into the season we're in – both the natural and metaphorical season of life – can help us live gentler, calmer lives.

As we notice patterns and rhythms of mood, energy, creativity, introspection, or cravings, we learn to better tend to our needs and love ourselves with less judgment. We become more attuned to and less fearful or resentful of the ebb and flow of life. We put down deeper, healthy roots of self-awareness and self-compassion that allow us to tilt and flex and not break when the storms come.

And we learn to mine for the achingly beautiful and sometimes heart-wrenchingly challenging gifts inherent in every season.

Krista xo

HOW TO USE THE JOURNAL

52 Mondays: Fall Session is meant to journey with you through 13 weeks of your imperfect and oh, so beautiful life and prompt you to notice what's happening in the natural world around you and in your inner world.

It is an invitation to read one short reflection as you start each fresh, new week and then to ponder or reflect on the practical application to your life as you move through the days ahead.

I have provided 3 journaling or reflection prompts you may choose to use to get your thoughts flowing but they are simply an invitation that you may prefer to leave aside.

I have left the pages undated and unlined as in addition to writing you may choose to doodle or sketch or Washi-Tape in little treasures you find that speak to you of fall.

Finally, at the end of the journal you'll find an opportunity to "rest, replenish, and review" as you consider the greatest lessons you've learned or what you've noticed about life and self in the past 13 weeks. This R&R&R exercise also asks you to identify what you need or want as you step awake and purposeful into winter.

I hope that this simple journal will surprise and delight you. I hope it serves as a gentle yet persistent reminder to tune in to the gifts of this season. And I hope that in even one small way you enter the next season stronger, more self-aware, or happier.

Krista xo

I am still becoming too.

HOLDING SPACE

There is a growing space
between you and I
and it feels a bit like grief.
A letting go
and making space
for you to become.
I am still becoming too.
Maybe one day
we'll find our way
back toward each other again.
And until then
I'll hold space for you
from over here.

Pause & Consider

1. What does it look and feel like to you to hold space for another?

2. Growth can feel messy and impact our relationships; will you hold yourself back or continue to forge ahead and let others choose their response?

3. Fall, like midlife, involves letting go or shedding and trusting there is good ahead. What are you being invited to let go of?

There are gifts to be mined in every season.

You're imperfect. Life is messy. Show up anyway.

There are gifts to be mined in every season.

You're imperfect. Life is messy. Show up anyway.

There are gifts to be mined in every season.

You're imperfect. Life is messy. Show up anyway.

There are gifts to be mined in every season.

You're imperfect. Life is messy. Show up anyway.

Fall is on its way.

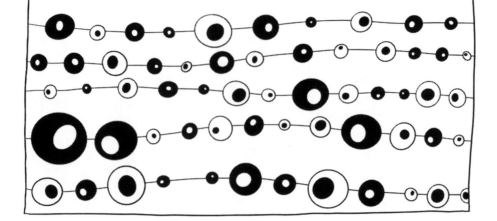

ANTICIPATION

The rain comes down steady. I open my windows wide – breathing in deep the dregs of summer and anticipating, slightly anxious, the cold, dark months ahead.

The changes come, slow and subtle, but my body feels them all the same. A little less light, a daub more grey. My right hand aches with cold some days though the temperature shift is slight.

Since its replacement, my hip no longer plays the barometer as it has since childhood but my body feels cold to the bone and shivers in anticipation.

Fall is on its way in the Northern Hemisphere and winter quick on its heels.

I love the flitting beauty of fall: the crunchy leaves and hand-knit scarves; happy gourds and the first frosty glitter. Who can resist the lure of homemade pumpkin-cashew lattes and long-simmered soups?

But if I am to weather well the long dark months of Alberta winter, I must thoughtfully prepare, nothing left to chance. My physical and mental wellness depend upon it.

I identify the tools and habits, the support I need, to stay mind-body healthy and then I relax into the shifting beauty of fall.

Pause & Consider

1. Are you affected by shifting light and temperatures? Check in a couple times a day with your body and your thoughts and notice what's coming up for you.

2. Seasonal living means living awake and responsive; what are the tools, habits, or support that will keep you healthy in this season?

3. Do you find yourself rushing through fall or do you take time to breathe it all in?

There are gifts to be mined in every season.

You're imperfect. Life is messy. Show up anyway.

There are gifts to be mined in every season.

You're imperfect. Life is messy. Show up anyway.

There are gifts to be mined in every season.

You're imperfect. Life is messy. Show up anyway.

There are gifts to be mined in every season.

You're imperfect. Life is messy. Show up anyway.

Bravery often looks like asking for help.

BRAVE

I was thinking about how for much of my life I felt I didn't quite belong and struggled to see where I fit in the world. Vulnerability was risky, more loss lurked around the corner, it felt safer to stay apart and figure things out on my own.

Yet bravery often looks like asking for help, risking rejection, advocating loudly for what we need or want. And I see now that what others think of me is not my business. I made the decision to love myself.

Never has perfection or having all the answers or knowing exactly how to navigate life's choppy waters determined my value or worth. And as I loosen my grip, open up to joyful possibility, as I put down strong roots of self-awareness and self-compassion, I find peace right here, in the middle of the storm.

I see that the safety of the boat has been an illusion and there is freedom and bravery in climbing out and stepping out upon the water.

Pause & Consider

1. Do you consider yourself brave?

2. What are you learning about yourself in this season; how can you apply that knowledge to handcraft a life that makes you proud?

3. Sometimes we need other people to remind us of our strengths and the gifts they see in us. Consider reaching out and asking a few people to remind you of the strength and bravery they witness in you.

There are gifts to be mined in every season.

You're imperfect. Life is messy. Show up anyway.

There are gifts to be mined in every season.

You're imperfect. Life is messy. Show up anyway.

There are gifts to be mined in every season.

You're imperfect. Life is messy. Show up anyway.

There are gifts to be mined in every season.

You're imperfect. Life is messy. Show up anyway.

I'm not wrong.

Neither are you.

YOU'RE NOT WRONG

I'm tired of making myself wrong.
I'm allowed to feel anger and be messy.
I'm permitted to bumble my way through marriage and parenting and
friendship,
giving and taking, doing my best, sometimes feeling ill-equipped for the task.
I'm allowed to put my needs and wants ahead of the pack
at least some of the time. More of the time.
I'm not wrong for struggling, questioning, or even choosing a different path
than yours.
I'm allowed to grow and change, to shift with the changing tide and season.
I'm OK if I see my gifts and all my struggle too and if I laugh about it
instead of tipping into judgment or shame.
I'm not wrong.
Neither are you.

Pause & Consider

1. Where are you judging yourself as wrong?

*2. Do you need a safe space to tell the truth about the reality of this season of your life?
Good and bad, it can be helpful to simply tell the truth about it all.*

*3. Do you notice yourself judging others as wrong because they're doing life differently
than you?*

There are gifts to be mined in every season.

You're imperfect. Life is messy. Show up anyway.

There are gifts to be mined in every season.

You're imperfect. Life is messy. Show up anyway.

There are gifts to be mined in every season.

You're imperfect. Life is messy. Show up anyway.

There are gifts to be mined in every season.

You're imperfect. Life is messy. Show up anyway.

Deep calling unto deep.

BEAUTIFUL

I used to think beauty looked like long lashes, a broad white smile, and a thigh gap. I used to think it sounded chipper and relentlessly positive. I used to believe beauty should make us feel inspired and content - like spring.

But now I think beauty's job is to cut deep and call us out into wild freedom or possibility.

I think beauty looks likes strength born of struggle, a fiery and determined spirit, a willingness to do hard things. I think it sounds like speaking up for what we believe in and truth-telling even when it's uncomfortable. It might sound like anger and an unwillingness to tolerate injustice.

At times beauty makes me feel things so intensely it hurts, to yearn for more, and calls me to walk in integrity even when I'm afraid.

The beauty of Autumn looks like scars and well-worn laugh lines, like a weathered soul and willing hand.

A battered sojourner who does not quit offering her light while she has breath within her.

A small wild-flower seeking light, determinedly, impossibly, through a crack in the concrete.

Or deep calling unto deep.

Pause & Consider

1. How do you define beauty in this season of life?

2. Do you see yourself as beautiful? What is one shift you can make to own your beauty?

3. In who or what do you see beauty modeled and what is it specifically that you see in them/it that you want or need?

There are gifts to be mined in every season.

You're imperfect. Life is messy. Show up anyway.

There are gifts to be mined in every season.

You're imperfect. Life is messy. Show up anyway.

There are gifts to be mined in every season.

You're imperfect. Life is messy. Show up anyway.

There are gifts to be mined in every season.

You're imperfect. Life is messy. Show up anyway.

I am enough.

I AM ENOUGH

I am strong enough to sit in the pain and sorrow that meets me on the path. In all the letting go of this season, I am strong enough.

I am ready enough to face what lies ahead without hiding and drowning and never coming back up for air. I am resilient and brave and ready enough.

I am capable enough to build a life of beauty and purpose as I forge ahead; it will be different from before and I may feel nervous. But I am capable enough.

I am open enough to mine for the gifts in this season, to scan for beauty, to choose my response. I will feel joy and taste pleasure and say yes to it all. Because I am open enough.

I am willing enough to see the full truth of who and how I am. To lay aside the disrespect and comparison and judging that keeps me bound. I am willing enough to do this work.

I am soft enough to love when it's hard and to make room for hope. To be wise and thoughtful and notice my tendency to run to protect myself. I am soft enough.

I am enough.

Pause & Consider

1. My life changed when I realized I am, indeed, enough as I am. Even if I desire healing or growth, I am enough right now. What do you think about this?

2. As much as fall has a bright and hopeful energy to it, the fall season of life can be fraught with challenging transition and soul-stretching work. Be gentle on yourself.

3. If you hold yourself and life to an impossible standard, what would it feel like to make space for "good enough"?

There are gifts to be mined in every season.

You're imperfect. Life is messy. Show up anyway.

There are gifts to be mined in every season.

You're imperfect. Life is messy. Show up anyway.

There are gifts to be mined in every season.

You're imperfect. Life is messy. Show up anyway.

There are gifts to be mined in every season.

You're imperfect. Life is messy. Show up anyway.

A call to go inward.

WAITING

I love fall - the electric charge of the air. The way it's easy and fun to plan and get organized, to store up for the long months ahead.

I love flickering candlelight and a fresh cool evening after an unexpectedly warm day. Wool cardigans and toques and crunchy red and golden leaves. An early, fleeting sprinkle of snow.

There is also a melancholy to fall - and I must admit I love this too. A call to go inward into nesting and introspection. To shift away from an outward, vibrant energy into a softer, inward turn of gaze.

The birds and squirrels come, making preparations for winter. They chatter at each other and sometimes I wonder if they're talking to me too. I listen carefully.

Though I don't fully understand, they speak to me of resilience and strength tangled up with the branches laid bare and days slowly surrendering their warmth.

I'm reminded that I chose to say yes to all of this. To all of life.

To welcoming and embracing sun and light but also darker nights. Diving all in to uncertainty and change, into transition and mystery. To quietly watching and expectantly waiting.

Pause & Consider

1. What do you love most about fall?

2. What do you notice about your hunger, moods, energy, and sleep patterns as you move through fall?

3. Consider collecting bits of fall's natural beauty and bringing them indoors. A fallen branch on the mantle, pinecones in a bowl; they can help us tune in to the beauty of the season.

There are gifts to be mined in every season.

You're imperfect. Life is messy. Show up anyway.

There are gifts to be mined in every season.

You're imperfect. Life is messy. Show up anyway.

There are gifts to be mined in every season.

You're imperfect. Life is messy. Show up anyway.

There are gifts to be mined in every season.

You're imperfect. Life is messy. Show up anyway.

I will be OK.

ON GRIEF

My parents were buried on bitter November days and as the calendar page turns, my soul begins to grieve. Even when I do not, it remembers. Grief is part of the cycle of things and I think it's only when we deem it bad or unwelcome that it causes a real problem. Separation is hard, and it's just as integral a part of life as celebrating joyful anniversaries or new life.

And so, we remember. We shed tears if they come and swap stories with those we love. Part of how I honor those who came before me is to write about them. As the years pass, the sharpness of pain subsides but the hole remains, and I use this awareness to offer encouragement to others. I offer back that which I have needed.

I glean from the seasons that have gone before and try to make sense of them and spin them with love into a gift that tells a story of light and hope. This is all that I have to give. And as the golden and red leaves fall and night comes quicker with each turn of the moon, I settle in.

I will be OK.

Pause & Consider

1. Do you notice that sometimes you aren't aware that you're approaching the date of a great loss yet your soul or spirit remember?

2. If you've said goodbye to someone you love, is there a way you'd like to honor them?

3. Western culture isn't good at making space for grief - but we get to decide for ourselves the way we process and what we need to heal.

There are gifts to be mined in every season.

You're imperfect. Life is messy. Show up anyway.

There are gifts to be mined in every season.

You're imperfect. Life is messy. Show up anyway.

There are gifts to be mined in every season.

You're imperfect. Life is messy. Show up anyway.

There are gifts to be mined in every season.

You're imperfect. Life is messy. Show up anyway.

The older I get the lighter I travel.

TRAVEL LIGHTLY

The older I get the lighter I travel.
I've released the heavy weight of comparison and not feeling good enough,
The baggage of trying to keep up and measure up,
Mental clutter that kept me distracted and waiting for someday.

The older I get the calmer I feel.
I've learned not to believe every thought my brain spins for me,
I can take responsibility for who and how I choose to be,
And tell the truth about what I want and need.

The older I get I laugh more freely.
I won't carry shame or guilt for just being me,
We're all imperfect and beautiful, doing our best,
A sense of humor is powerful medicine as we forge ahead.

The older I get the better I love you.
I love myself so have more to give you,
I see your strengths and the light you carry,
And see us both as gifted and worthy.

The older I get the better I listen.
I'm less threatened now and listen more than I speak,
I'm rooted and strong, open to your perspective,
Hungry to meet face to face in the messy middle.

The older I get the lighter I travel.

Pause & Consider

1. How do you feel about aging?

2. When we feel rooted and calm we can more easily hear others. Are you rooted?

3. What do you want to let go of so you can "travel lightly"?

There are gifts to be mined in every season.

You're imperfect. Life is messy. Show up anyway.

There are gifts to be mined in every season.

You're imperfect. Life is messy. Show up anyway.

There are gifts to be mined in every season.

You're imperfect. Life is messy. Show up anyway.

There are gifts to be mined in every season.

You're imperfect. Life is messy. Show up anyway.

Change comes softly.

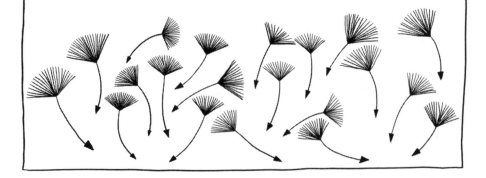

EYES AND HEART WIDE OPEN

Every mistake is a lesson about what does and does not serve you well.

Every friendship, even those that don't last, a gift in season.

Every risk taken is a decision to taste life and not allow fear to control your every move.

Each new dawn is a gentle call to receive with gratitude, to breathe deeply, to pick up joy.

Every loss ushers in a season of intense grief and remembering the importance of loving well in the moment.

Every single hug, even those with sticky fingers, is a chance to pause and lean in and to quiet the frantic to-do list in your head.

The physical pain is an opportunity to choose rest, practice self-compassion, finally grasp that joy and pain can coexist.

Each open door you choose to walk through is a chance to offer your gifts and practice holding the outcome loosely.

That painful challenge in your life can be a prodding to ask for help.

The addiction or illness or recurring situation might just be an invitation to stop running and numbing.

The moments when we realize that we have grown and healed remind us that change comes softly, often when we're not looking.

Pause & Consider

1. What might change in your life today, or what might you hear, if you begin living eyes and heart wide open?

2. Whose voice are you listening to the most these days?

3. What are you learning in this season?

There are gifts to be mined in every season.

You're imperfect. Life is messy. Show up anyway.

There are gifts to be mined in every season.

You're imperfect. Life is messy. Show up anyway.

There are gifts to be mined in every season.

You're imperfect. Life is messy. Show up anyway.

There are gifts to be mined in every season.

You're imperfect. Life is messy. Show up anyway.

If only...

ON CREATIVITY

I never thought of myself as creative.
I played the flute
and dabbled with oil paints,
made homemade cards,
and some of my own clothes,
but I definitely wasn't creative.
I cooked and baked from scratch,
grew herbs and veggies in a tiny plot of soil,
joyfully concocted balms and salves in my kitchen.
I sewed simple curtains and pillow covers,
made crafts with my little people,
and shared a love of art and words with them.
I wished I was creative.
We listened to Bach and Beethoven,
set up drums in the living room,
hunted down a used piano and money for lessons.
We watched bugs and birds
on nature walks
and sketched what we saw.
We admired the art in beautiful children's books.
But I was not creative.
I built a business brick by brick,
as I launched creative and wise kids into the world,
and offered up tentative words of my own
to help you feel seen and heard.
If only I were creative.

Pause & Consider

1. Isn't it interesting how limited our viewpoint can be while we're in the thick of life? Time and perspective can help us witness a more honest, fuller picture of who we are.

2. I now believe we're all creative at the core - how are you expressing your creativity these days?

3. Are you having fun? Are you making space for dabbling, playing, being a beginner, making joyful messes?

There are gifts to be mined in every season.

You're imperfect. Life is messy. Show up anyway.

There are gifts to be mined in every season.

You're imperfect. Life is messy. Show up anyway.

There are gifts to be mined in every season.

You're imperfect. Life is messy. Show up anyway.

There are gifts to be mined in every season.

You're imperfect. Life is messy. Show up anyway.

Help me live
clear and calm
in every season.

INTENTIONAL HABITS

There are a handful of core practices I've carried with me over the years which help me live clear and calm in every season.

The first is identifying, and writing on a sticky note that I check in with regularly, 3-5 descriptors that reflect how I want to be in the world. I take personal responsibility for how I show up.

The second is to bookend my days with gratitude. The science on this is clear and I've felt the difference it makes to me to live committed to noticing all the gifts of life.

Third is a no-bullying policy I instituted many moons ago. I speak to myself kindly, respectfully. Bullying never brings about positive, sustainable growth or healing, and I'm modeling strength and health to my children.

The fourth habit is to nourish my body like I matter. To drink clean water and eat whole foods, to enjoy purposeful treats without shame. To move and sleep and take time to breathe.

Fifth, I honor my natural desire to dream and plan but I loosen my grip on a precise outcome. I keep my eyes on a bigger vision while staying open to shifting course and iteration.

Pause & Consider

1. Would one of these habits serve you?

2. Self-awareness is essential for building a right-sized life. Use this next week to take notes about your energy patterns, what makes you happy, your inner dialogue, and/or do some reading around personality.

3. Is there a disconnect between what you say you want and how you live your days?

There are gifts to be mined in every season.

You're imperfect. Life is messy. Show up anyway.

There are gifts to be mined in every season.

You're imperfect. Life is messy. Show up anyway.

There are gifts to be mined in every season.

You're imperfect. Life is messy. Show up anyway.

There are gifts to be mined in every season.

You're imperfect. Life is messy. Show up anyway.

I choose to be still.

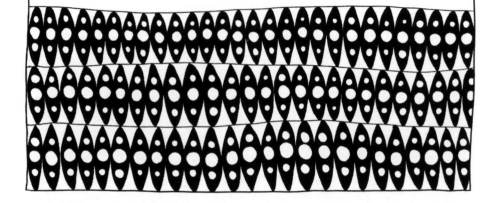

BE STILL

I bought a new sign that sits on my fireplace mantle - it reads "be still."

I need this reminder to quiet my anxious mind and heart. To remind me to rest.

To see and feel that I am safe in this moment. Loved. Held. And though not everything in my life feels easy or resolved, in this exact moment all is well.

I don't have to see the end or have all the answers. But I can take one step. Tomorrow I will take another.

And I will trust. I will trust my wisdom, I will trust that I've walked through storms before and we always come out on the other side. I will trust in the miraculous, mystery of life.

In fall, I need this reminder in a big way. It's easy for my heart and mind to lose the joy of today as I consider the cold, dark, and starkness that lies just around the corner.

I can miss the glorious, breath-taking beauty of this season because I'm afraid of what's next.

I choose to be still.

Pause & Consider

1. What does this make you think or feel - "be still"?

2. We're afraid of dying or aging, of kids leaving the nest, of rejection and plans failing and maybe never meeting someone to love. Is fear robbing you of the joy of what is?

3. What if the bulk of our pain and suffering is the result of not being mindful and present in each moment?

There are gifts to be mined in every season.

You're imperfect. Life is messy. Show up anyway.

There are gifts to be mined in every season.

You're imperfect. Life is messy. Show up anyway.

There are gifts to be mined in every season.

You're imperfect. Life is messy. Show up anyway.

There are gifts to be mined in every season.

You're imperfect. Life is messy. Show up anyway.

Rest

Replenish

Review

Consider the greatest lessons you've gleaned about life or self in the past 13 weeks.

Where do you notice yourself struggling or meeting with ongoing resistance?

You're imperfect. Life is messy. Show up anyway.

*Consider the greatest lessons you've gleaned
about life or self in the past 13 weeks.*

Identify what you've done well at and where you're proud
of yourself for how you've show up to life.

There are gifts to be mined in every season.

Consider the greatest lessons you've gleaned
about life or self in the past 13 weeks.

What do you most need or want as you step awake and purposeful
into the next season of life?

BETSY HUGGINS

About Betsy

Krista has been my coach and cheerleader for over a year now. I found her at a time when I was searching for answers, and her words spoke to me in a very meaningful way. Through her incredible understanding of the human spirit I have started to recognise, and respect my own natural strengths and struggles.

I am not a writer, yet through Krista's writing I have learnt what it means to communicate. We all have thoughts and stories we use to make sense of the world, but we all also have our own ways of expressing these thoughts. Mine is a messy mixture of making things, with lines and with pixels. Krista's words light a spark in my soul that inspires me to try to make sense of my own stories in a creative way.

These doodles you see in this journal are those. Expressions of thoughts and feelings that have been inspired by Krista's words. Simple, and honest. I hope Krista's words, and possibly my drawings, inspire you to go on your own journey inside, as I believe the gifts you will uncover are priceless.

With love,
Betsy x

If you want to say hello, I'd like that, I'm on Instagram @tinygiantlife